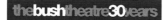

The Bush Theatre presents
the world premiere of

Untouchable

by Simon Burt

Directed by Natasha Betteridge
Designed by Martin Reynolds
Lighting Design by Tanya Burns
Sound Design by Scott George for Aura Sound Design Ltd.

3 – 21 December 2002

Cast

Lou   Samantha Robinson
Manni   Pooja Shah

Director   Natasha Betteridge
Designer   Martin Reynolds
Lighting Designer   Tanya Burns
Sound Designer   Scott George for Aura Sound
                                 Design Ltd.
Deputy Stage Manager Sarah Hunter
Set Construction   Andy Latham Scenery

Press Representation   The Sarah Mitchell Partnership
                               020 7434 1944
Marketing Consultation Sam McAuley for Chamberlain
                               McAuley 020 8858 5545
Advertising and Graphic M & H Communications
Design   020 7412 2000

The Bush Theatre would like to offer special thanks to Rebecca Callard, Mark Rosenblatt and Sunetra Sarker.

Very special thanks to Jenny Worton from Simon Burt.

This performance lasts approximately 80 minutes with no interval

This play received its world premiere at The Bush Theatre on 5 December 2002

At The Bush Theatre

Artistic Director	Mike Bradwell
Executive Producer	Fiona Clark
General Manager	Jane Grater
Literary Manager	Nicola Wilson
Development Manager	Kate Mitchell
Production Manager	Pam Vision
Chief Electrician	Matt Kirby
Resident Stage Manager	John Everett
Assistant General Manager	Alex Mercer
Literary Assistant	Owen Lewis
Box Office Supervisor	Dominique Gerrard
Box Office	Janet Kumah
Front of House	Kellie Batchelor
	Caroline Beckman
	Johnny Flynn
	Muzz Khan
	Delores Kumah
	Kate Ryan
Associate Artists	Biyi Bandele-Thomas
	Es Devlin
***Pearson Writer in Residence**	Shelley Silas
Sheila Lemon Writer in Residence	Isabel Wright

*The Bush Theatre has the support of the Pearson Playwright's Scheme sponsored by Pearson plc.

The Bush Theatre is the winner of The Peggy Ramsay Foundation Project Award 2002

Samantha Robinson – Lou

Samantha graduated earlier this year from Rose Bruford College, where she won the 2001 Laurence Olivier Bursary Prize. Her theatre work there included Gillian / Rose / Rachel in *Behind The Scenes At The Museum*, Cinderella in *Into The Woods*, and Jesse in *The Bright and Bold Design*. Other theatre includes Audrey in *Little Shop of Horrors* (Preston Playhouse Theatre); Alice in *Closer* and Brooke in *Popcorn* both for the Barefoot Theatre Company, and Annabel / Monica in *Send In The Clown* (Jermyn Street Theatre). She recently made her professional debut as Morwenna May in *Song of The Western Man* at the Chichester Festival Theatre. Samantha has just made her television debut playing Lucy in *Final Demand* (BBC), and recorded Lizzie in *Everisto's Epitaph* for BBC Radio 4.

Pooja Shah – Manni

Pooja was a member of the Finchley Youth Theatre where her theatre work included *Light In The Village*, *A Midsummer Night's Dream*, *Song For A Dark Queen* and *Wyrdsisters*. Her professional roles include Meena in *Bend It Like Beckham*, *Holby City*, *Suzie Gold*, Sinjata in *Is Harry On The Boat*, *Jesus The Curry King* and *Love Bites* (Channel 4).

Simon Burt – Writer

Simon Burt was born in 1975. He studied drama at Loughborough University 1994–97 and attended writing classes with the Royal Court Young Writers Programme 1999–2000. He was nominated by The Bush Theatre for a place on the 2001 Performing Arts Lab Writing For Younger Audiences Workshop. *Untouchable* is his first produced play.

Natasha Betteridge – Director

Natasha Betteridge is Artistic Producer for the Northampton Theatres Trust for whom she has directed *The School for Scandal*, *House and Garden* and *Barefoot in the Park*. Natasha is also an Associate Director of the West Yorkshire Playhouse where she has directed *Mister Heracles, Visiting Mr Green*, *Stig of the Dump*, *Kes*, *Lettice and Lovage*, *Rita, Sue and Bob Too*, *The Life and Times of Young Bob Scallion* and *An Appetite for Living*. Other theatre credits include the premiere of *A Listening Heaven* by Torben Betts (Stephen Joseph Theatre, Scarborough). She was also director for three seasons of new writing at The Orange Tree Theatre Room, including world premieres of *Clowns* by Christina Reid, *Death of an Elephant* by Trevor Preston and *October Song* by Andy Hinds. Other directing credits include *The Dock Brief* and *Edwin* (Oxford Playhouse and world tour) and *Yerma* (Royal National Theatre Studio). Natasha is a founder member of Welsh-based Thin Language Theatre Company, for whom she co-directed *Forever Yours Marie-Lou* and produced *Nothing To Pay* (Wales/London tour) and *Badfinger* (Donmar Warehouse).

Martin Reynolds – Designer

Martin studied architecture at the Bartlett School of Architecture, UCL. Martin has a design practice in the East End of London, which combines projects with research, collaborations and teaching. Current projects include a residential house in Dalston and an exhibition at the Imperial War Museum in Manchester. Collaborations include a kinetic installation for performance artist Graeme Miller and a photographic exploration into domesticity with artist Mary Lemley. Previous collaborations range from a sound-scape in Salisbury with Graeme Miller to a building proposal for London's South Bank with artist Richard Wilson and Architects McCormick Jamieson Pritchard. Martin teaches design in London.

Tanya Burns – Lighting Designer

Tanya was awarded the prestigious Arts Foundation Fellowship for Lighting Designers in 1996, and has since gained her MSc in Light and Lighting at UCL's Bartlett School of Architecture. In addition to theatre, she is now a lighting consultant on exhibition, architectural and environmental projects. Most recent work includes: Nasdaq TV Studios, Times Square New York; Coca Cola at Madison Square Gardens, New York; Samsung Pavilion and Exhibition at the Winter Olympics, Salt Lake City (International Gold Award Winner). West End credits include: *Hay Fever* (Savoy); *You'll Have Had Your Hole* (Astoria); *Funny Money* (Playhouse); *The Killing of Sister George* (Ambassadors) and *September Tide* (Comedy). Also in London: *Blackbird* (The Bush); *Been So Long* and *Cockroach Who?* (Royal Court); *Mules* (Royal Court and Clean Break); *Red and Another Nine Months* (Clean Break); *Ballad of Wolvoo* (Gato); *All For Love* and *Solitude of the Cotton Fields* (Almeida); *Saltwater Moon* and *Miss Julie* (Kings Head). Other work includes: *When We Were Married* (Leicester Haymarket); *Present Laughter* (Birmingham Rep); *Singing In The Rain* and *Macbeth* (West Yorkshire Playhouse); *Crimes and Crimes, Monsch Meier, Artificial Jungle, Playboy of the Western World, One Small Step, 42nd Street, Hedda Gabler, East, The Thirst, Thru the Leaves, Decadence* and *The Caretaker* (Leicester Haymarket); *Dead Meat* (West Yorkshire Playhouse); *Candida* (Plymouth Theatre Royal); *School For Scandal* (RSC, Stratford and Barbican); *Fantastic Voyage* (Edinburgh Festival) and *Soundbites* (Almeida and ENO Opera Festival). Dance includes *Headshot* (V-Tol Dance Company, The Place and tour).

Scott George – Sound Designer

Scott began working in sound in Australia, and has since brought his skills to almost every continent in the world. Recent design credits in England include: *Sive* (Druid Theatre, Galway); *Cabaret* (Chichester Festival Theatre); *Kosher Harry* (Royal Court); *Maria Friedman In Concert* (West End); *The Taming of the Shrew* (Nottingham Playhouse); *Bali, Death Of A Salesman, Dolly West's Kitchen, Peter Pan* (Haymarket Theatre, Leicester); *A Buyer's Market, A Carpet, A Pony & A Monkey* (co-design with John Leonard at The Bush); *Journey to the West* (Tara Arts); *The Lost Musicals* (Royal Opera House); *Much Ado About Nothing* (London International Festival at The Guildhall); *The Three Musketeers* (Young Vic). Production Engineering credits include: *Benefactors* (Tour / West End); *The Distance From Here* (Almeida); *Macbeth* (Ludlow Festival); *Saturday Night Fever* (British tour); *Lulu, Coriolanus / Richard II* (Almeida at Gainsborough Studios, also New York and Tokyo); *Macbeth* (RSC tour); *Plenty* (Almeida at The Albery). In July 2000, Scott became Show-Control Director of Aura Sound Design Ltd.

30 Years of The Bush Theatre

The Bush Theatre opened in April 1972 in the upstairs dining room of The Bush Hotel, Shepherds Bush Green. The room had previously served as Lionel Blair's dance studio. Since then, The Bush has become the country's leading new writing venue with over 350 productions, premiering the finest new writing talent.

Playwrights whose works have been performed here at The Bush include Stephen Poliakoff, Robert Holman, Tina Brown, Snoo Wilson, John Byrne, Ron Hutchinson, Terry Johnson, Beth Henley, Kevin Elyot, Doug Lucie, Dusty Hughes, Sharman Macdonald, Billy Roche, Tony Kushner, Catherine Johnson, Philip Ridley, Richard Cameron, Jonathan Harvey, Richard Zajdlic, Naomi Wallace, David Eldridge, Conor McPherson, Joe Penhall, Helen Blakeman, Lucy Gannon, Mark O'Rowe and Charlotte Jones.

The theatre has also attracted major acting and directing talents including Bob Hoskins, Alan Rickman, Antony Sher, Stephen Rea, Frances Barber, Lindsay Duncan, Brian Cox, Kate Beckinsale, Patricia Hodge, Simon Callow, Alison Steadman, Jim Broadbent, Tim Roth, Jane Horrocks, Gwen Taylor, Mike Leigh, Mike Figgis, Mike Newell and Richard Wilson.

Victoria Wood and Julie Walters first worked together at The Bush, and Victoria wrote her first sketch on an old typewriter she found backstage.

In 30 years, The Bush has won over one hundred awards. Bush plays have transferred to the West End and Broadway, and have been successfully adapted for film and television. Bush productions have toured throughout Britain, Europe and North America.

Every year we receive over fifteen hundred scripts through the post, and we read them all. According to The Sunday Times:

'What happens at The Bush today is at the very heart of tomorrow's theatre'

That's why we read all the scripts and will continue to do so for at least another 30 years. We hope you'll be here too.

Mike Bradwell
Artistic Director

Fiona Clark
Executive Producer

Coming Soon

14 Jan – 15 Feb

Paines Plough in association with
The Bush Theatre present
the London premiere of

The Drowned World

by Gary Owen

Directed by Vicki Featherstone

A vicious tale of love, revolt and beauty. How far would you go to save your own skin?

'And that is why we can't have these fatally radiant creatures walking round the place…reminding us how clumsy and mean spirited and graceless and cowardly and shapeless and flabby and foul we all are'

Winner of a Fringe First and hit of the Edinburgh Fringe Festival 2002

Book online at
www.bushtheatre.co.uk
(no booking fee)
or call
020 7610 4224

Support The Bush

The Bush Theatre is a writers' theatre. We commission, develop and produce exclusively new plays. In addition to reading every script sent in, we commission up to seven writers each year and offer a bespoke programme of workshops and one-to-one dramaturgy to develop their plays. Our international reputation of 30 years is built on consistently producing the very best work to the very highest standard.

The search for new voices and the quest to reach as wide an audience as possible is ongoing. It is an ever-increasing challenge. We gratefully acknowledge support for our core programme from London Arts and London Borough of Hammersmith and Fulham. However, there are many individuals and companies whose generous support enables us to maintain and expand the programme of writer's development and continue to reach new young voices.

The Bush Theatre is launching a new **Patron Scheme** to coincide with its 30th Birthday season. The new scheme will offer opportunities for both Individual and Corporate Giving. Participating patrons will be able to enjoy a close relationship with the theatre in addition to receiving a wide range of benefits, which will include ticket offers and invitations to special events. This new scheme will directly support the Writers' Development Programme and help produce the new writers and new plays of the future.

Please join us in supporting another 30 years of new theatre. For full information on the **Patron Scheme**, please call Kate Mitchell, Development Manager on 020 7602 3703.

Gold Patrons of The Bush Theatre

The Agency, Giancarla Alen-Buckley, Jim Broadbent, Nick Cave, Joe Conneely, Feelgood Fiction, Ken Griffin, Albert & Lyn Fuss, Jonathan Green, Mary Hoare, ICM, ltnetwork.com, Catherine Johnson, Roy MacGregor, The Mackintosh Foundation, Michael Palin, Ralph Picken, Universal Pictures, 6th Floor Ltd, Richard Wilson, William Morris Agency (UK) Ltd, Working Title Films, Richard Zajdlic

Patrons of The Bush Theatre

Alan Brodie Representation, Alexandra Cann Representation, Conway, Van Gelder, Gillian Diamond, Paola Dionisotti, Charles Elton, Chloë Emmerson, David and Yvonna Gold, David Hare, Amanda Howard Associates, Philip Jackson, Peter Kelly and Karen Duggan, Primary Stages Theatre, New York, Marmont Management, Tim McInnerny, Stephen Nathan and Colleen Toomey, Samuel French Ltd, Rochelle Stevens & Co, Lady Warner, Richard Warner

The Bush would like to extend special thanks to the following for their support: The Mathilda and Terrence Kennedy Charitable Trust, The Olivier Foundation. This theatre has the support of the Pearson Playwrights' Scheme, sponsored by Pearson plc.

First published in 2002 by Oberon Books Ltd.
(incorporating Absolute Classics)
521 Caledonian Road, London N7 9RH
Tel: 020 7607 3637 / Fax: 020 7607 3629

e-mail: oberon.books@btinternet.com
www.oberonbooks.com

A catalogue record for this book is available from the British
Library.

ISBN: 1 84002 319 8

Cover photo: M + H Communications

Printed in Great Britain by Antony Rowe Ltd, Chippenham.

Characters

MANISHA/MANNI
Asian descent, seventeen years old

LOUISE/LOU
white, seventeen years old

Note

The following script was correct at the time of going to press but may differ slightly from the play as performed.

Setting is present day in Wakefield, West Yorkshire. We are in the part of the city where all the night-clubs are based.

Set in a bed-sit for one. There is a very small kitchen area, cooker, fridge, sink and very small preparation surface. A rickety table. A three-quarters-sized bed. Little cupboard space. A horrible old wardrobe. The place is not overly-falling-to-pieces, just a bit neglected and too small for two people.

MANNI is strong-willed, determined, academically ambitious. Underneath she is hopelessly inexperienced in just about everything, but especially relationships and large quantities of alcohol. She idolises LOUISE.

LOUISE is fiery, lives for the moment, but lacking direction and any kind of overriding passion. She is far more experienced than MANNI, but she still can't understand what she wants from life. Hedonism seems to be her only option. She cares intensely about MANNI.

Scene 1

There is a large unopened suitcase between table and bed. On table is a large cardboard box.

LOUISE wears casual clothes, jacket on. She is knelt on bed looking out of window. We can hear the noise of a busy city street beyond. LOUISE looks up and down the street. She comes away, shutting window. Sits on end of bed looking around room kind of amazed. She lays back on bed and tries bouncing up and down on it using only back-muscles. Sits up, testing springs with hands.

LOU: Not bad. Not bad at all.

On her knees LOUISE bounces up and down on bed joyfully.

Oh yeah! Me and you are gonna have a lot of fun.

LOUISE looks at the bulky suitcase. Looks at watch.

Come on Manni, what you doing? I want my stuff an' all! God! You can't have your tongue that far up me Mam's arse. Where are ya?

Giving in to temptation LOUISE opens suitcase and pulls out a couple of MANNI's clubbing dresses and pulls not-very-impressed face at them.

Bloody hell fire Manni. No wonder you never see any. Go dear me what a –

LOUISE leaves dresses and suitcase, looks into cardboard box on table. She reaches in and pulls out an ancient black and white portable television. LOUISE slaps it down on table.

Bloody hell fire. Go dear…like something outta the ark that is.

LOUISE looks back in box. She starts to pull more stuff out.

Ah! What have we here?

LOUISE pulls out a load of text books, files and folders. LOUISE looks at first book.

Oh Manni Manni Manni, so fucking dedicated aren't you? 'Introduction To Psychology.'

LOUISE looks at each book before slapping it down on table.

(*Half-singing/chanting this.*) I'm not doing you any more. Not doing you any more…any more… (*Blows a big fat raspberry at one book.*) …any more, any –

LOUISE gets to last book, stops.

Never ever did you an' you can fuck off all same.

LOUISE goes to shelves to put books onto. Looks at shelf, looks at books, looks round room and –

Nah.

LOUISE puts the books on the floor by the door, puts a nearly full vodka bottle on the shelf where books would have gone. Nods, pleased with herself. Looks at watch again.

Manni! Fuck's sake come on!

We hear front door open and shut, MANNI puffing and panting. LOUISE darts out into corridor.

Here here, give 'em here.

LOUISE re-enters lugging two impossibly large suitcases, leaves them only just in the doorway.

MANNI (casual clothes) follows close behind utterly exhausted, almost wheezing. She has to squeeze through the suitcases LOUISE has left. MANNI collapses onto bed, very heavy breathing, gasping, wheezing. LOUISE sits beside her, looking down at her.

Aye Manni! Manni! We done it! We out, we up. Wakey!… Manni? Up Wakey…Manni, you alright there?

MANNI: Oh… Oh…

LOU: What?

MANNI: …Oh aye.

LOU: Oh aye what?

MANNI: Oh aye I'm alright.

LOU: You sweating cobbs there you know…ta for getting me stuff…were me Mam there? You didn't need me key then?… You get it all? Me dresses?

MANNI puts hand up in protest. LOUISE waits moment, desperate to speak.

Soz… Tips haven't come thru yet which is a right bugger but Friday they say. That'll be alright though cos weather's been right good, beer garden chocka wi' folks an' sproggs stuffing faces, loads a tips, loads for me anyway I reckon. So Friday's still on for doing Wakey large day. Aye Manni? Manni!

MANNI: Good…good…good job I…I haven't got no shift on tonight. Couldn't be standing up…right knackered. Right bloody knackered I am.

LOU: You be alright. What you like? Bloody soft.

MANNI: I am soft, I'm martyr to me'self I am lugging your crap…and that were after telling my folks I moving out an' lugging my stuff so I were already knackered!

LOU: How'd it go with your folks?

MANNI: Oh you wouldn't believe it if I told you.

LOU: Thought they'd be alright your folks?

MANNI: They're devastated.

LOU: What? You leaving home and you didn't think they weren't gonna be devastated? What your folks?

MANNI: Well yes an' no I –

LOU: Just told mine and went. Did deed, told 'em me an' you got this place and were out of the door in thirty second.

MANNI: I couldn't do that.

LOU: So you got tears? I bet yer Dad were blubbing all over.

MANNI pushes herself up onto her elbows.

MANNI: Oh aye. From me Dad like you wouldn't believe. Not me Mam, very stoical is me Mam, but me Dad, set me off. The reassuring that went on, still studying for uni, I had to promise over and over and I can go back anytime I like. Not that I will but you know.

LOU: What 'bout yer brother?

MANNI: Bagsied me room and were moving in 'fore I'd left.

LOU: Bastard... Like I say, just told mine and went.

MANNI: They fine with that?

LOU: Didn't stay long enough to find out did I? You know more than me.

MANNI: Do I?

LOU: Aye! You been there...are they?

MANNI: What?

LOU: Fine?

MANNI: ...I wouldn't like to say.

LOU: Didn't think you would.

MANNI: Sensitive people parents.

LOU: But yours hate me.

MANNI: Aye they do. Blame you for me going.

LOU: You don't have to say!

MANNI: But you know that's what they'd think.

LOU: But you don't say it.

MANNI: Soz.

LOU: God. Mine love you, mine fucking love you...

MANNI: Soz.

LOU: Mine wonder what I'm doing with little miss A-levels here.

MANNI: Hate you.

LOU: Hate you more.

MANNI: Aye up hang on – she says pop round for yer tea if you like. Yer Mam says.

LOU: Oh! Just remembered that have you?

MANNI: I'm still knackered – gimme mo.

LOU: So me Mam not taking it funny like?

MANNI: Even more stoical than my Mam your Mam. I wouldn't like to say, but she does say pop round for yer tea.

LOU: She's said that to make me feel all… God, thanks for getting me stuff. I couldn't be doing wi' me Mam.

MANNI: You're alright.

LOU: Aye I am. An' now we up Wakey –

MANNI: Up Wakey!

LOU: Aye! Now we up Wakey I am gonna fix you up with someone really really nice, who'll fuck your brains out!

MANNI: No no no no no no!

LOU: No! No more no no no noing! Leave it all to me. That's my job.

MANNI: No! Just a beer aye? Buy me a beer?

LOU: Manni! You up Wakey now!

MANNI: I am aren't I?

LOU: Aye!

MANNI: No it's my Mehir I want to, you know, with…my Mehir I…you buy me a drink for getting yer stuff an' we fine an' dandy.

LOU: But you and Mehir are gonna?

MANNI: Now I'm up Wakey? Oh aye.

LOU: You want something to drink now?

MANNI: Aye, I could –

　– LOUISE goes to get vodka bottle as –

　I could murder a tea.

　LOUISE, rolling eyes, goes to one of suitcases and opens it, rummages through a bit panicky and then hurriedly opens other one. Inside them is a mess of belongings.

LOU: You get it all?

　MANNI starts to push herself fully back up – recovered.

MANNI: Think so.

LOU: Me dresses? You get me dresses?

MANNI: It were heavy enough.

LOU: So where me dresses?

MANNI: I think they're there, but...

LOU: What?

MANNI: You could always you know...

LOU: What?

MANNI: Wear one a' mine?

LOU: Fuck off.

MANNI: What's wrong with them?

LOU: You can't see ought.

MANNI: You can see me knickers.

LOU: Barely.

MANNI: I like to give their imagination something to work with, works with my Mehir.

LOU: You haven't fucked your Mehir, or ought.

MANNI: Yeah but –

LOU: You haven't fucked!

MANNI: Yes I know that but –

LOU: You haven't! So how's it working? What scale of measurement are you using here?

MANNI: …Me own.

LOU: I don't believe this…what else have you forgotten? You were gone ages.

MANNI: Well we had a pot of tea. Gotta be sociable haven't you, and I get on with your Mam so –

LOU: You said you wouldn't like to say about me Mam an' now it turns out you been having pot of fucking tea with the bitch? Suppose you had piece of fucking Battenbury an' all didn't you?

MANNI: …It's nice yer Mam's Battenburg.

LOU: All comes out now don't it? So come on what did she say about me then?

MANNI: Nothing Lou. Nothing. Nothing at all.

LOU: So what did you talk about?

MANNI: Just me A-levels really.

LOU: What she say about me dropping outta college?

MANNI: Nought. Nothing to me.

LOU: It were only some intermediary hotel services shit. Right cut into my pub shifts that did…shit it were…she not say ought about it?

MANNI: No.

LOU: No?

MANNI shakes head.

Wish she'd given me right slagging, least you know where you are with a slagging… She said nought?

MANNI: Lou nothing, she even helped me pack your things…

LOUISE looks hurt.

…that didn't come out right…

LOU: That why me dresses aren't here! I knew it. The bastard bastard bitch – you let her?

MANNI: What'm I meant to do? She's yer Mam.

LOU: I knew you wouldn't get 'em.

MANNI looks into nearest suitcase, reaches down and pulls out one of LOUISE's (significantly skimpier than MANNI's) dresses, holds it up knowingly taking LOUISE aback a moment…

You…you…

MANNI: Aye? Aye?

MANNI tosses dress at LOUISE who catches it.

LOU: What you like?

MANNI: I sneaked 'em in 'fore she snaffled 'em away, she tried but I got 'em.

LOU: You fucking wind-up merchant you. Hate you.

MANNI: Hate you more.

LOUISE dives over suitcase and belongings to give MANNI tightest hug.

Alright alright!

MANNI tosses rest of dresses at LOUISE. During following talk LOUISE is stuffing her clothes into drawers. After a moment MANNI starts to do same with her belongings, far slower and more delicately.

LOU: God you wind up – God, now you are going to get hooked up with someone Manni, I promise you, someone really really nice who'll fuck yer brains out!

MANNI: No no. Beer beer. Yeah? I'm happy with beer.

LOU: Beer can lead to –

MANNI: No no.

LOU: Alright I'll whisper to your Mehir to finally finally fuck your brains out? You'd like that wouldn't you? You'd lurve that.

MANNI: No no no no no no…

LOU: But it's Mehir Manni? You're you know, in…you know…luuurrvvee!

MANNI: I know, I could be like but whoa please Lou. I believe you can do what you say you can do but please aye? No no.

LOU: That a yes?

MANNI: No! I'm begging you!

LOU: You begging me?

MANNI: Aye I am, I'm begging you – don't! I don't want to fuck his brains or fuck ought out.

LOU: Fuck your brains Manni, yours! Fuck his. Come on Manni, you up Wakey wi' me now, you gotta get hang of this.

MANNI: Do I?

LOU: Aye! God, I mean God – don't you ever just want to have someone so like now! Now in the club bog like. Get it out of your system?

MANNI: I hate you.

LOU: Hate you more.

MANNI: Look…thank you –

LOU: Aww! Don't go all fucking polite on me!

MANNI: No, thank you for the set-up offer. But I just couldn't enjoy me'self if I knew you were organising… I'll start wi' beer alright? Now I'm up Wakey I'll have more beer.

LOU: Look wear one of my dresses, even your Mehir'll get idea then won't he? Wear one of mine.

MANNI: No!

LOU: Go on! You'd look stunning.

MANNI: That what I'm worried about.

LOU: Then go on, this weekend.

MANNI: No no.

LOU: Manni!

MANNI: Louise!

LOU: Manisha!

MANNI: No!

LOU: For me?

MANNI: No!

LOU: Please!

MANNI: No!

LOU: Wouldn't you like to?

MANNI: …Yeah.

LOU: Go on!

MANNI: No!

LOU: …Wuss.

MANNI sees where her books have been put.

MANNI: You put me books there? They gonna be safe there?

LOU: They be fine.

MANNI ponders this for a moment and then decides to let it go.

MANNI: You not got monk on with me have you?

LOU: …No.

MANNI: I do like your dresses…you know Mehir said he'll finish wi' me if we took this place?

LOU: Did he?

MANNI: Aye. And I've ignored him haven't I? I'm here aren't I?

LOU: Yeah.

MANNI: But I'm not like you Lou. I couldn't ever be like you.

LOU: Aye.

MANNI: I'm more, much more one step at a…you know?

LOU: He hasn't finished with you?

MANNI: Oh no. I'd have said wouldn't I?

LOU: Aye… Awww, he's a sweety is your Mehir. Though he's gonna fuck himself in head if he thinks his lust has an on/off switch. Though it's dead sweet of him to threaten you like that…no one threatened me like that.

MANNI: They will…so we here, up Wakey like we always said.

LOU: At last.

MANNI: So we gonna do Wakey?

LOU: What tonight?

MANNI: Are we?

LOU: It mid-week Manni. Can't do big night mid-week. Bit dead. Bit sad you know.

MANNI: Sad?

LOU: Aye!

MANNI: But can't we?

LOU: Well there's places open bit like but…bit and you know. Anyway first night here should be right special.

MANNI: So just quiet drink me and you?

LOU: No we saving it. We're building up to the biggest piss-up ever, 'til next Friday like, it be with Susan, Shreela and lasses and everyone. Yeah? You up for that?

MANNI: I'm up for that!

LOU: Don't have to be home by anytime, back here and me and you see night away.

MANNI: But not 'til Friday?

LOU: Build-up is everything.

MANNI: We just gonna watch telly?

LOU: Telly? An' your crap telly an' all wi' no Sky, no box office? No we not! No, tonight we gotta bond as room mates. Bed mates really. So Chinese and –

MANNI: What you getting at bed mates?

LOU: There only one bed.

MANNI: Aye.

LOU: What? Aye nothing like that neither.

MANNI: No!

LOU: No! What I mean is –

LOUISE picks up vodka bottle.

MANNI: Oh.

LOU: Yeah?

MANNI: Yeah…no, no I don't understand.

LOU: Manni! We've no shifts 'til tomorrow night, this is our home now isn't it?

MANNI: Our home. That's nice.

LOU: So we stay up all night just talking.

MANNI: Talking?

LOU: Yep. All night. You ever done that?

MANNI shakes head.

Haven't you?

MANNI: No.

LOU: You not lived Manni.

MANNI: I haven't.

LOU: I done it with Susan and Shreela.

MANNI: Where were I?

LOU: Home by midnight like a good girl. I always wished you were there cos you talk about stuff different like and they don't, an' Susan and Shreela – cliquey. But tonight it just me and thee and we keep going 'til we watch sun rise over Argos Superstore…then we flake.

MANNI: All night? What we talk about?

LOU: Crap mostly…you up for it?

MANNI nods as LOUISE hands her vodka bottle and heads for door.

I'll go get us a Chinese yeah?

MANNI: Aye, prawn crackers?

LOU: Lots of.

MANNI: Cuppa tea?

LOU: Fuck the tea.

LOUISE is gone. MANNI alone, looks at vodka bottle nervously, then pulls out another of LOUISE's skimpy dresses, looks at dress even more nervous.

✴ Scene 2

It is shortly before dawn. MANNI and LOUISE are both sat on the bed (in dressing-gowns) either side of window looking out. The remains of the take-away litter the bed and floor. A fair bit of the vodka has gone. Both are nicely drunk, not pissed, just nicely drunk. However MANNI is feeling it more. They sip their drinks throughout.

MANNI: Quiet isn't it?

LOU: Yes it is.

MANNI: Can't get over how quiet it is. Never seen Wakey so quiet.

LOU: What time is it?

MANNI: Just gone four.

LOU: Sun be coming up soon. My favourite time of day this is, so fucking fantastic. Everyone asleep. No one can get at you. You're so tired you can talk a load of crap about world peace and believe it.

MANNI: We haven't talked about world peace.

LOU: Saving that for 'nother time.

MANNI: Plenty more of those to come.

LOU: Aye.

MANNI: I reckon I done really well.

LOU: Aye, you lasted course.

MANNI: No, I mean Mehir. I hardly mentioned him.

LOU: Well you have but –

MANNI: Do you think me and Mehir will?

LOU: What?

MANNI: Shag?

LOU: Shag? What's wi' you been all vulgar like? Your Mam an' Dad won't care for that.

MANNI: Alright, making love.

LOU: That's Manisha.

MANNI: But do you?

LOU: What's it matter what I think?

MANNI: It matter to me cos you me bestest mate.

LOU: Aye, I am.

MANNI: Cos I reckon it is a relationship we having, me an' him, I want you to know it is.

LOU: Alright, fine.

MANNI: No offence to you Lou like, but it not just about having relations like. An' it not just going out, it been four month now.

LOU: Alright I dunno. I'm pissed, don't listen to me I – aye hang on. There is something I want to know about him.

MANNI: Go for it.

LOU: You said he'd got monk on with me and you living in here? What that about?

MANNI: Just being monky.

LOU: But what 'bout?

MANNI: Cos of sharing bed thing.

LOU: That just money that is – bit tight I know.

MANNI: The money?

LOU: The bed! But sixty quid all in, bargain isn't it? More money for up Wakey.

MANNI: What I said, I said that.

LOU: Maybe we should get a fold-up though, if we wanna stretch some nights.

MANNI: He said I weren't showing commitment, sharing bed wi' you like.

LOU: Fuck's sake what's he on, me an' you only topping an' tailing.

MANNI: I said that.

LOU: So why's he – God. I mean have you even talked about shagging?

MANNI: Well yeah, kind of but he's…he's…

LOU: What?

MANNI: …He wants it to be right and stuff he says.

LOU: Oh for – I be honest with you here Manni, I think he's playing with your head.

MANNI: Do you?

LOU: Aye.

MANNI: How?

LOU: Arrrghh!!!

MANNI: No no no no why?

LOU: Why? Cos I think Mehir is a good boy who before he'll show you his willy he'll have to take you home to show mummy and daddy and put that little ring on your finger all good and proper. And even then you'll have to put light out, and he'll be dead quiet and dead dedicated and dead proper and treat you like a lady at all times, but he'll never change a nappy. See how I keep using word dead?

MANNI: That isn't gonna happen. He knows it isn't.

LOU: Does he?

MANNI: Aye! What's he think I'm doing up Wakey wi' you?

LOU: I dunno, what are you? I'm pleased like but –

MANNI: Look me an' him we got ages, there's no rush. And me and you here, this is me first step to getting outta here.

LOU: Outta where?

MANNI: Wakey.

LOU: Oh.

MANNI: I mean what me Mam and Dad have done like is
  great, they own their own house an' everything but they
  haven't had chances I've had, I want better, you know?
  Want more, do it better, for them too. It's nought against
  them but, you know what I mean? Yeah?

LOU: No. With my folks they done it all. Less I become a
  chuffing millionaire.

MANNI: Why don't you?

LOU: Nah. I'm up Wakey.

MANNI: Yeah but what you gonna do?

LOU: I think of something.

MANNI: My first step this. An' it more than worth putting
  up wi' one of Mehir's sulky monk ons, but then…but
  then I love him. I do. We're like –

  *MANNI shows LOUISE two crossed fingers. LOUISE laughs
  and sticks a V-sign back at MANNI who isn't impressed.*

  Shurrupp!

LOU: You're a sad soft saft un' you.

MANNI: You know my Mehir's frightened of you?

LOU: Me?

MANNI: Aye, you cos, cos of lots of things but cos, well
  cos you see what it is, what it is is he seems to think
  once me and him have made love I'll blab everything
  about him to you.

LOU: Yeah. Course you will. What's the sad bugger expect?

MANNI: I know, but it's a big issue with him.

LOU: Quite normal.

MANNI: In a way it's your fault we haven't.

LOU: My fault? I'm gonna fucking bray him if he don't shurrup wi' this crap.

MANNI: No no he hasn't said it's your fault, that's me just talking crap but…but he is scared of ya.

LOU: Manni, Manni, haven't you ever thought, he might just be scared of you?

MANNI: Me?

LOU: Yeah. He'll say ought will your Mehir if he's you know, tentative.

MANNI: What's wi' the long word?

LOU: Oi you cheeky mare! You were asking! Always fucking Mehir these days – hate you.

MANNI: Hate you more… Soz Lou, but I reckon it really is me and you together he finds too much. Why can't he like you, and why can't you like him aye? I mean why?

LOU: Shit happens Manni, get over it.

MANNI: Be lovely if you did.

LOU: Aye! I been here longer, I got history with you, he should respect me first as yer best mate, not other way round.

MANNI: Aye you're right, you right cos we've been together while me and you haven't we? I mean forever like.

LOU: Aye, nine years.

MANNI: But maybe, maybe we key into each other in a way that maybe others find a bit, you know…

LOU: No I don't. What you gonna say here?

MANNI: Well we might, we might come across a bit stone-masonish like.

LOU: You saying cliquey? We're not fucking cliquey.

MANNI: Hate you.

LOU: Hate you more…we're not. We're not – fuck 'em! Fuck 'em all! We untouchable me and you.

MANNI: That nice.

LOU: Aye, an' if people can't, me and you – they not worth …not worth shite you know?

MANNI: Nine years though Lou.

LOU: And best is yet to come. We're gonna do Wakey 'til it can't stand no fucking more. Toast! Toast to doing Wakey.

They toast 'Doing Wakey!'

Cos you see we gotta face it Manni, we're still gonna be comparing arses me an' you long after we joined blue-rinse brigade.

MANNI: Have I ever pointed out a nice arse to you?

LOU: …No. You haven't.

MANNI: I haven't lived…what's a blue rinse? That to do wi' arses?

LOU: No it isn't!

MANNI: What's that then? That soon?

LOU: No! Me gran were one.

MANNI: That all me and you got to look forward to?

LOU: What?

MANNI: These blue rinse people?

LOU: Time to flake, time to flake. Getting silly.

—LOUISE looks back out.

Sun's coming up.

MANNI: Oh it is, aww! Look at that.

LOU: Which side you want?

MANNI: Umm…

LOUISE can't be bothered to wait while sozzled MANNI decides and so crawls under duvet taking side nearest the wall – which will be her side.

LOU: If me dreamings disturb ya gimme kick.

MANNI: You'll kick me back.

LOU: And don't hog fucking duvet, you right hog meister you.

MANNI: Why we have to top n' tail? Could be same end like.

LOU: That's couple like. We're not a couple like.

MANNI: We untouchable like.

LOU: We topping an' tailing!

MANNI: Only thinking 'bout yer feet.

LOU: I don't mind yer feet, just wanna sleep.

MANNI: I mind yours…look!

LOU: What?!

MANNI: Only take a mo…I know done thing this time of morning is talk bollocks but I really really mean I, I can't 'magine ought coming 'tween me and you. Can't. You're right, we're untouchable, and it not crap it's true. It's true.

LOU: Sleep tight Manni.

MANNI: Sleep tight Lou.

MANNI crawls under the duvet. ~~Quiet,~~ moment passes.

LOU: Your feet do stink.

MANNI: An' yours…aye Lou!

LOU: What?

MANNI: We up Wakey!

LOU: We up Wakey.

MANNI: Roll on Friday.

LOU: Patience my young apprentice, build up is everything.

~~Another quiet~~ moment passes. MANNI darts out of bed and out of door.

What now?

MANNI: Need bog!

Bathroom door slams shut.

LOU: Like I'm gonna rush in and watch.

✗ Scene 3

Late evening.

Window is wide-open. Music from nearby clubs flooding into room. There are various trendy alcoholic bottled drinks strewn around. Duvet is all screwed up.

LOUISE is sat on floor (in her significantly skimpier than MANNI's clubbing outfit), sipping end of bottled beer and calmly smoking a cigarette, having a very mellow moment.

The room door is open and from beyond we hear front door open and close and MANNI's voice. Soon as LOUISE hears MANNI she bolts up and hurriedly tidies, straightens the duvet – during which MANNI can be heard…

MANNI: You're having a laugh. Aye, doss house place this is Shreela. Every Friday from now on like this, aye I'll have it done in big flashing lights 'bove door. Yeah we'll dance night away me and Lou.

LOU: Ha! No fucking chance. Bloody knackered.

LOUISE sits back down with fag and beer being all mellow again. MANNI enters (in her black clubbing dress), speaking down mobile in one hand, bottled beer in other.

MANNI: Oh yeah. Twenty-four hour party me an' Lou.

LOU: I'm bloody knackered!

MANNI: Aye that's her ladyship calling…alright. Call us tomorrow, aye, and do Wakey tomorrow? Great!

MANNI turns phone off and tosses it onto bed. MANNI wanders bit aimless.

LOU: Twenty-four hour party?

MANNI: What you been up to?

LOU: Nought special.

MANNI: What you like? …Can I?

MANNI slumps next to LOUISE, beckons for cigarette. LOUISE passes it, MANNI takes quick drag. Passes it back.

I could get used to this.

LOU: That's idea.

MANNI: Now that, that was a darn good tip top turvy wurvy night Lou. Did Wakey!

LOU: Oi!

MANNI: What?

LOU: You can calm it bit you know. Mehir not about now.

MANNI: Not cos of him.

LOU: Bullshit it is.

MANNI: Isn't.

LOU: Well did you then?

MANNI: No. He gone home.

LOU: Well what did you do?

MANNI: We had a bit of monk on with each other at start like.

LOU: Yeah I saw, what that about?

MANNI: You. Don't worry, him been monky. But after that we danced together for ages and ages…and kissed, kissed ages.

LOU: Sad.

MANNI puts hand to head, clearly pretty drunk. Steadies herself on table and sees bed. She frowns and stares intently at bed for a moment. She looks at LOUISE a moment (who doesn't meet her gaze) suspicious.

MANNI: What you been up to?

LOU: Stuff…

MANNI: What? In here? In bed? …Think I might be chundering.

LOU: You gotta learn how to pace yerself.

MANNI: I can't be doing wi' the chundering.

LOU: Then don't fucking drink!

MANNI: But I like the drink, no I've an essay due Monday, I haven't time for the stuff after the drinking.

LOU: I haven't got any essays due or ought. I can chunder much as I like.

MANNI: But not in here.

LOU: Weren't planning on.

MANNI: My college stuff in 'ere, on chunderfest frontline SO YOU BE CAREFUL!

LOU: Oh shut up you daft drunk mare. What do you think I'm gonna do? Anyway aren't you gippy? Chunder on 'em yerself you will…

MANNI: Alright alright…toast!

LOU: Toast to what?

MANNI: To…to…ahhh! Toast what?

LOU: To keeping it down!

They toast, clink, 'Keeping it down!'

MANNI: God, we done it Lou, we did Wakey.

LOU: Nought gets past you.

MANNI: But we did yeah?

LOU: Yeah, yeah. You know if you'd have told me, just a month ago like, that we'd be here in centre of town I'd …I'd…I don't know…I just wouldn't have.

MANNI: Dream come true.

LOU: Aye, you not gonna cry are you?

MANNI: Just welling you know?

LOU: What you like? Beautiful end to a beautiful evening.

MANNI: Beautiful end? I got my beautiful Mehir swimming round in here? I won't get to sleep. Gotta carry on, dance, watch sun come up.

—LOUISE shakes head and groans.

LOU: No.

MANNI: No?

LOU: I just wanna flake. I mean this is great, so great.

MANNI: Aye.

LOU: No I don't mean how you mean, I mean no freezing me tits off waiting for taxi. And no rowing with me Mam about time, hem lines…contra you knows…it's great This has been best night ever.

MANNI: You said it were nought special?

LOU: Not in a Wakey way. Me Mam would never have let me out in this.

MANNI: …No.

LOU: Got it with me tips. Not me wages, just me tips! You wanna take on more shifts Manni, you really do.

MANNI: I'll think about it.

LOU: Wi' your college summer hols up soon, eight week, get shifts in, tips you'd get Manni, you wanna get one like it…you do.

MANNI: I'll think about it.

—MANNI has gotten a bit tearful, wipes eyes with arms, embarrassed.

LOU: Bloody hell Manni, you are pissed.

MANNI: No no, your Mam wouldn't let you out wi' aggro, my Mam wouldn't full stop…but if I pestered me Dad he'd let me, he would even though it break his heart me going out like that – not that there's ought wrong in you going like cos it's you you know but, me Dad he would, long as I were happy…he were so upset when I left.

LOU: He be alright now.

MANNI: I know. I been daft. But me Dad, all I do is hurt him.

LOU: No you don't. You're just drunk and talking balls. Dads are, God, you know my Dad still thinks I haven't, right pisses me Mam off cos she knows.

MANNI: You know before I knew I were gonna be a psychologist for about two week before I were gonna be a lawyer. I said to him I were and he were so pleased, he brought home loads of bumpf about it. He thought it cos of that I changed me mind but I didn't but he'll have thought…

LOU: …Look, he want you to be happy wouldn't he?

MANNI: Yeah.

LOU: You happy here?

MANNI: Oh aye.

LOU: Then come on, get that finished! Get it down you!

MANNI: You said I had to pace myself!

LOU: …Get it down you!

MANNI finishes the beer in one big swig.

We happy now?

MANNI nods.

MANNI: Ta for getting me drinks. Good of ya.

LOU: You educated girls, you haven't got the disposable income of us working girls have you?

MANNI: Pay you back.

LOU: Don't worry about it. Do it all again tomorrow?

MANNI: Aye.

LOU: Time to flake. Shift tomorrow.

MANNI: No no no no no no no!

LOU: No!

MANNI: No! Stay up all night. Dance. Watch sun.

LOU: I can't.

MANNI: You no staying power you.

LOU: A-hu?! You saying I no staying power?

MANNI: I am!

LOU: Have you got any idea who you're talking to here cos them fighting words those Manni, them dangerous fucking fighting words!

MANNI: Aye!

LOU: You don't wanna do this.

MANNI: What you like Lou? What you like? What you like?!

LOU: Alright! Bring it on!

MANNI: The bar is open!

LOU: Aye, forget kipping. We don't even have to go out to get that club atmos.

LOUISE wanders towards the light switch by door. Still got beer and starts to dance. MANNI gets off bed and copies LOUISE's dancing.

Are you so pissed I can get you to mosh?

LOUISE does a little moshing. MANNI copies her, far more energetically.

Well gone.

LOUISE flicks light switch off. The room is bathed in the murky glow of an orange street lamp with flashes of colour from a nearby club. Both start to dance with more energy, circling each other, going back to back, MANNI sliding her back up and down LOUISE's.

MANNI: This is what I did with Mehir.

LOU: I don't wanna know.

MANNI: Up…and down –

LOU: Manni! I not Mehir!

MANNI staggers to bed and to the window shouting out –

MANNI: Mehir – I'm gonna shag you! I'm gonna gonna!

Suddenly MANNI seems to give up, flake, and flops out on bed, completely still. Oblivious, LOUISE dances the night away.

⚹ Scene 4

Early morning. Window open. We hear traffic outside. Duvet isn't there.

MANNI is laid far side from bed on floor, curled up asleep with only a towel laid over her. She is in her black clubbing dress.

We hear LOUISE's voice from down corridor.

LOU: I'll see you later then…yeah it's been…yeah. Alright, bye.

We hear door close. LOUISE wanders back into room wrapped in the duvet. She is carrying a little post which she ignores and tosses onto table. Looks wistfully round room, off in a little world of her own. Sees MANNI asleep on floor and nearly freaks.

Manni! What the fuck you doing down there?

MANNI stirs a little.

MANNI: What's it bloody look like. Trying to get some bloody kip!

LOU: You pissed?

MANNI: Aye!

LOU: I mean drunk.

MANNI: Aye!

LOU: You pissed angry aye?

MANNI: Aye!

LOU: You going to work?

MANNI: I don't think so. You cover for me?

LOU: Not chundering! Manni I covered for you three, four times last ten days – you're wearing their patience…I…I thought you were going back to Mehir's, you were getting on great.

MANNI: We were.

LOU: What happened?

MANNI: Kissing, he said night and he went.

LOU: …I wouldn't have brought anyone back, if I'd have known…well not to stay all night.

MANNI: Wouldn't you?

LOU: No! I never heard you come back. Why didn't you say?

MANNI: You and him! In there! What you fff – think?!

LOU: What'd you do?

MANNI: What it look like? Me back's killing. And it were you who went on about getting fold-up bed!

LOU: Come on, get into bed. I'll do you brekkie, something really nice.

MANNI: We nought in.

LOU: Okay, I'll pay for slap-up fry-up at café.

MANNI: Will you put in hole and shut up?

Groggy MANNI gets up and stumbles to bed, changes mind about getting in and just sits on end. LOUISE fusses in middle of room, unsure what to do, just stands there…

Need bowl Lou.

LOU: Aww! You not chundering again Manni!

MANNI: Bowl!

LOUISE rushes to get bowl (with duvet wrapped around her).

Quick! Quick!

LOUISE rushes back with bowl and pases it to MANNI who sits with it on her lap, facing partly down into it should she feel the need. LOUISE just stood in middle of room wrapped in duvet. Looking a right lemon.

LOU: You've got some post.

MANNI: What is it?

LOUISE opens it.

LOU: Uni prospectus.

MANNI: Where?

LOU: Kent.

MANNI: Oh aye...

LOU: What?

MANNI: I'm going on trip there in few week, wi' college, to have look round like.

LOU: Oh...long way away Kent isn't it? ...Further than London that is. Isn't it?

MANNI: Will you sit down?

LOUISE doing as she is told sits on end of bed wrapping duvet round herself. Flustered. Embarrassed.

LOU: I...I didn't keep you awake...later on, did I?

MANNI: Should you have done?

LOU: I didn't know you were there.

MANNI: No I know you didn't.

LOU: Oh no.

MANNI: Aye, what I were thinking that when you were doing...that.

LOU: God – fucking Mehir!

MANNI: Don't go blaming him.

LOU: I am blaming him, fucking eunuch! Way you an' he were going on even I thought –

MANNI: Lou!

LOU: Manni come on! It's a crush. A totally monogamous chemical crush. Yer body's having laugh on yer.

MANNI: You what?

LOU: You never trust yer body.

MANNI: Don't you?

LOU: No! And it's pathetic.

MANNI: Me?

LOU: Yeah you, you right clever, loads of get up and go and you after a no-hoper like Mehir and his delivery van. You right better than him, wasting yer'self…what?

MANNI: And what did you talk 'bout in dead of night after yer fuck fest eh? What were you telling him cos I heard ya, you wishing you had your own Mehir and then him yakking on 'bout his ex and you right listened him go on and on and on you did. Couldn't believe ya! So desperate, and you call me sad you sad cow!

LOU: …I want to see him again. Happens you know.

MANNI: Well lay off me and Mehir then, I wouldn't have let on at all if you'd left off…what were you doing 'fore talking?

LOU: Not telling you now.

MANNI: Sounded nice, what were it?

LOU: …You'd like it.

MANNI: Nice was he?

LOU: Oh aye.

MANNI: Seems nice.

LOU: He is.

MANNI: That's nice.

LOU: But I don't care 'bout him like – you should have woken me up! I'd have kicked his arse out!

MANNI: Would you?

LOU: Why won't you believe me?

MANNI: Maybe we should think about getting fold-up bed like you said.

LOU: No!

MANNI: No I think –

LOU: No no! It won't happen again. I promise ya!

MANNI: We should get a fold-up.

LOU: No!

MANNI: You wanted one in first place.

LOU: Not cos of this.

MANNI: Well I'm not having another night like that.

LOU: You won't have to kip on floor again. I promise.

MANNI: Look I know it's what you been thinking.

LOU: What?

MANNI: I know what you think. You got me paying my share of bills and rent and at same time sleeping on fold-up listening to you and your studs fucking away. I'm just subsidising your fuck-fest! But that's alright, I get to be up Wakey and be wi' you. It's alright –

LOU: It not like that!

MANNI: It alright. I won't feel so bad about bringing Mehir back here – and don't you think it won't happen.

LOU: You taking piss wi' that? I laugh at that, I laugh right in face of it!

MANNI: Lou!

LOU: Half that bed's mine and I'll shag on my side if I wanna, an' out of courtesy to you cos I'm polite I won't shag no one while you're in bed – including you!

MANNI: Lou – it's not you, it what cat drags back in, and, and I…I keep having to lie in it.

LOU: You haven't said ought up to now.

MANNI: I don't like causing waves. But you not doing it on fold-up, that be mine!

LOU: I'll have you know I can manage alright without a bed cos I got imagination I have – you can hitch your skirt up with your bum on sink and… (*LOUISE looking at the tiny kitchen area.*) …balance one foot on fridge and… I can see that working.

MANNI looks mortified, in a hungover kind of way.

MANNI: I can't tell what you say. Whether you been serious or – JUST DON'T! Not in the bed aye? House rule! No shagging in bed!

LOU: For all you know I could be shagging me'self in there, in bed every night and you don't know a thing. I'll have you there every night listening for every creak and fumble and –

MANNI: LOU DON'T!!!

LOU: I'm fucking surprised I don't hear you wanking every night way that bastard's wound you up tighter than – or are you right quiet?

MANNI looks completely embarrassed and buries her head in plastic tub, as if trying to burrow right down into it.

Oh Manni, I sorry I sorry. I, I didn't – Manni, Manni…

LOUISE rushes to sit with MANNI, rubs her back as MANNI rides out a potential chunder-wave. MANNI recovers. LOUISE continues to comfort her.

MANNI: …Can't tell what you mean. You just…I see what your Mam has to put up with, lot of patience your Mam.

LOU: Don't you bring her into it.

MANNI: She alright your Mam.

LOU: Aye! Don't go saying ought here you can't take back.

MANNI: Sorry.

LOU: When I said about the fold-up I did mean I like to stretch, nought else! It difficult wi' you in there an' all, like wandering ivy you are, and you don't know where you're putting your stuff, I like to stretch.

Awkward silence. LOUISE just looking ahead annoyed and embarrassed, MANNI with head back in bowl. LOUISE stands and goes back to table, sees papers on table, looks at them.

See you got essay back.

MANNI: Oh…yeah.

LOU: Shit mark that is. That isn't gonna get into any uni. Must be crappest mark you ever got.

MANNI: Rub it in why don't you?

LOU: That won't get you into Kent uni. Don't make habit of it. I got high hopes for you.

MANNI: It's Friday today isn't it?

LOU: Yeah.

MANNI: Weekend. We doing Wakey?

LOU: Aye, course.

MANNI: Til it can't stand no more?

LOU: Aye. Another try at Mehir?

MANNI: Hate you.

LOU: Hate you more.

MANNI: No, no Mehir. Me and you do Wakey like we keep saying we will. No pissing off with Mehir or…or anyone right?

LOU: Me and you. That'd be good.

MANNI: …I'm gonna get a fold-up.

Scene 5

A Friday night again. Window a little ajar, muffled club music filling room.

There is a fold-up bed the opposite side of the table to the proper bed.

MANNI enters in her black clubbing dress. Carrying a Hooch she sups out of. She's a bit tearful. Stands in middle of room unsure what to do. Looks across to window and goes to push it open. Clear music fills the room. MANNI sups from bottle, finishes it.

Sees vodka bottle and picks that up. Unscrews cap, has a bit. Sits on end of bed holding vodka, trying to control her tears. Carelessly wipes nose with length of her bare arm.

LOUISE enters in one of her clubbing outfits just in time to catch the nose wiping.

Stands in doorway, clearly a bit hyped up.

LOU: Gross Manni!

MANNI: Sorry. Ya weren't meant to see that.

    LOUISE goes and closes window, dulling the music.

LOU: Bit early to be hitting vodka like that isn't it? Bit early to be back here too isn't it? Even for you these days?

MANNI: Been bit of a bad evening.

LOU: Mine's been bag of cack an' all.

MANNI: That why you back? ...I don't need to go on fold-up? God, I never needed to go on fold-up, what were point?

LOU: Like I would wi' you in 'ere?

MANNI: You did few week back.

LOU: That were an accident.

MANNI: You and him over then?

LOUISE nods.

That be what? Two and half week, that yer longest?

LOU: Nearly.

LOUISE gestures for the vodka bottle, drunken MANNI doesn't twig.

Hello? Can I have it yer hog meister?

MANNI: Sure. One mo.

MANNI (rather over the top) takes swig of vodka, wipes mouth.

LOU: Ahhh! The pupil becomes the teacher.

MANNI passes bottle to LOUISE who takes a smaller swig, feeling no need to show off anymore.

MANNI: So why's yours been cack? Lou? ...Lou?

LOUISE has gotten bit tearful.

Never tell me ought these days.

LOU: What's to tell? You see me all time.

MANNI: Isn't same. Where you been?

LOU: Where you think I been?

MANNI: You have been with your fella? …Nice?… Where?
…In bog? …Were it nice?

LOU: Ho-hum.

MANNI: Ho-hum? That it?

LOU: What else you want me to say?

MANNI: You never say fantastic or phwoarh or ought,
just…alright.

LOU: When it's more than ho-hum or alright you'll be first
to know, I promise you…you not pissed are you?

MANNI: I'm head fucked pissed.

LOU: Fuck's sake! Susan an' Shreela, I told 'em not to get
you pissed – you be chundering again?

MANNI: No it weren't them. I wanted to. I really wanted to.

LOU: Good for you Manni, good for fucking you.

MANNI: Aye.

LOU: You'll lose ya job, already fucking your marks up and
for what?

MANNI: A laugh.

LOU: What laugh? Chundring?

MANNI: It is a laugh. Like you have.

LOU: But I keep it together. I keep it down.

MANNI: Keep what together? You don't do ought.

LOU: I aren't getting into this Manni. I don't care. I gotta flake. Long fucking afternoon shift tomorrow. Think of the tips aye? Think of the tips.

MANNI gestures for the vodka bottle.

MANNI: Lou?

LOU: Huh?

MANNI gestures, LOUISE passes it, MANNI has swig, wipes mouth whilst –

MANNI: Lou, when you gonna get excited about something?

LOU: 'Bout what?

MANNI: 'Bout anything. You used to get right excited about Wakey. You never get excited no more, not even 'bout Wakey.

LOU: What am I meant to get excited about? This is me life.

MANNI: A bloke?

LOU: A bloke?

MANNI: Well yer job then, something.

LOU: I work behind a bar Manni.

MANNI: But it's a nice bar and you're up Wakey like you always wanted.

LOU: Aye! I'm up Wakey!

LOUISE is all tearful.

MANNI: Lou?

MANNI goes to put drunken arm round her friend. Doesn't help, MANNI offers vodka bottle, LOU shakes head, MANNI shrugs and has swig herself.

LOU: Me bloke, we didn't fuck.

MANNI: Oh?

LOU: Didn't wanna, not like that no more… I only wanted to talk to him…'bout stuff, 'bout ought, 'bout life like an'…

MANNI: What?

LOU: He laughed. At me.

MANNI: Why?

LOU: Him an' his mates. Going on 'bout birds wi' gobs on 'em, and laughed…cos I'm just hilarious me aren't I? …so I threw his beer over him.

MANNI: Lou!

LOU: I know I know. I'm a twat.

MANNI: But you said he were nice.

LOU: He was. Good too. Real… I mean he were a good fuck.

MANNI: That's what you mean.

LOU: Aye, that's what I mean isn't it?

MANNI: What? It is what you mean isn't it?

LOU: …Yes.

Tears from LOUISE and she takes bottle off of MANNI, takes swig.

MANNI: Lou?

LOU: That night here, wi' you on floor, I told him stuff I hadn't told no one, not even you. I wanna kick me own head in, stuff I were telling him…

MANNI: I only caught bits. Tiny tiny bits. The bit about Mehir, that's all.

LOU: Aye Mehir. After we'd fucked for first time I said how much I wanted what you and Mehir have got…

LOUISE gets exasperated by herself, her face boggling almost trying to understand herself, arms outstretched as if miming asking the ultimate question.

I mean, I mean…what exactly have you and Mehir got?

MANNI: (*Shrugs.*) Dunno.

LOU: Neither do I! …but I want it! And I told him…I told him I don't know what to do, about ought to do with me. I not a fucking clue what, who I am. I'm nought.

MANNI: You me best mate Lou.

LOU: I can see him laid on pillow in our bed him thinking sucker. I don't know him, don't owe him anything of me, couple of hours…I would have told him more…ought! What'm I like eh? Hadn't even been drinking. Not head-fuck drinking what's me excuse?

MANNI beckons for vodka, takes swig.

Manni! You had enough!

MANNI: You not heard why yet.

LOU: Oh just tell him to –

MANNI: No it isn't that.

LOU: It's Mehir isn't it? Should be used to it by now.

MANNI: Can you let the Mehir thing go just once Lou?

LOU: You said you had cack evening! Means him don't it?

MANNI: Not everything I do revolves round him you know.

LOU: Whoa! Complete world view change there.

MANNI: Lou!

LOU: What?

MANNI: He's proposed! …Aye.

LOU: As in marriage?

MANNI: Aye, marriage.

LOU: …Bastard.

MANNI: I thought we really really really really really were and…

LOU: And what?

MANNI: I were saying about uni, I got a trip to look round Kent coming up next week and I said how we'd cope with long distance. Maybe I only go to Leeds but –

LOUISE is twirling her hand, a kind of Get-on-with-it! gesture.

He don't want me to go.

LOU: On the trip?

MANNI: To uni. Ever.

LOU: Oh aye? What a surprise there.

MANNI: Said we couldn't…you know.

LOU: I…there's a word for this an' it isn't pretty…what is it? I use it a lot, oh yeah: emotional blackmail.

MANNI: And then he proposed.

Pause. MANNI takes further swig as LOUISE gapes at her.

LOU: And this is marriage right?

MANNI: Yeah.

LOU: Not engagement like?

MANNI: Marriage.

MANNI takes another swig, LOUISE continues to gape.

LOU: ….bastard. That emotional extortion that is. What a shit bastard thing to do. You're not gonna –

MANNI: I haven't said no yet.

LOU: But you're not gonna –

MANNI: Like you I dunno. I dunno ought.

LOU: You dunno? You better start not dunnoing!

MANNI: Well I do know I wish he hadn't, I so wish he hadn't.

LOU: Okay. That's a good start.

MANNI: He should have kept his gob shut, I know that… but I love him…twat… Says he's nearly twenty. Should be settling down. All I wanted him to do was be there. Be him. He couldn't even do that. Had to open his mouth and say something… An' I were so looking forward to all the different stages like, like you're meant to get in relationships. Do each stage to the max…we had it all to do.

LOU: You want a cig? I want a cig.

MANNI nods, LOUISE passes cig and lights it. MANNI passes LOUISE vodka who has swig and nurses bottle. MANNI puffs away on cig.

MANNI: That's good. I'm giving up you know.

LOU: You no chance. Turning into right pro you are.

MANNI: Come on Lou, you know, you known for ages. Cos you smart you are, not like stupid thick me.

LOU: An' what's that?

MANNI: What you said 'bout him been a good boy! Being dead! When he looks at me, he don't see me when he looks at me, does he?

LOUISE shakes head slowly.

No, I don't bewitch him or torment his soul or any of that shite. He don't see me beyond the clubs round here. Even me body don't do ought for him and he's meant to have a cock. I mean what is he? Some kind of freak? They're not meant to be able to control themselves.

LOU: Huh! Tell me about it.

MANNI: I just thought he might see in me what I do in him…but that just sounds dead wanky don't it…so…I just want him to shag me. That's all.

LOU: So, see in you then, what does he see?

MANNI: You know!

LOU: No what is that? Come on!

MANNI: What I reckon he sees?

LOU: Yes!

MANNI: I don't have to tell you.

LOU: Don't you?

MANNI: No! He…in me he sees perfect form of his parents' wishes don't he?

LOUISE just nods.

Marriage, mortgage, business, kids, routine, respect, soon. I want him to fantasise about me. I want to feel his imagination run all over me…what's wrong wi' wanting that?

LOU: But you never put your cards on table like you did.

MANNI: But what 'bout –

LOU: No! You don't be all doey-eyed like cos then some bastard marriage man like Mehir goes 'Oh hello!'

MANNI takes vodka bottle, swigs.

MANNI: I don't want it like that.

LOU: There are some nice ones who are in it just for the shagging.

MANNI: No, I'm gonna say it, love. That's what I want. Not the freaky planet he's on where I give up all my exams, all my future to raise his kids. They should be an optional extra if all else goes according to plan not a fucking starting point. Fucking twatting bastard we've not even fucked yet and he presumes to…me…bastard. Well at least I know now and I'm fucking angry, and I don't half know what I'm fighting for now.

LOU: What?

MANNI: …Stuff!

LOUISE beckons for vodka bottle, swig.

LOU: How'd you leave things?

MANNI: Told him I'd think it over – I'm not gonna.

LOU: I don't care, you haven't said no have you?

MANNI: No.

LOU: You are not!

MANNI: …No.

LOU: Manni!

MANNI: I won't!

LOU: Right I'm gonna go see your Mam and Dad. I might be satan in a frock to 'em but they'll know it case a' better the devil you know!

MANNI: Lou!

LOU: Well will your Dad want you marrying or even getting proposals off a' likes of him? Aye? Bloody worst nightmare for them I bet, yeah? What they think of him?

MANNI: They think he's alright.

LOU: Do they?

MANNI: No, they think he's a twat too. Me Mam even said the word.

LOU: Twat?

MANNI: Aye.

LOU: Your Mam? You'd right upset yer Dad, devastate, distraught him it would!

MANNI: I know Lou alright! But when I say no, that's it isn't it? For me an' him? He'll never, you know?

LOU: Yeah.

MANNI: Yeah. I need to get used to idea, that all. I won't say yes.

LOU: But will you say no?

MANNI: …Yes.

LOU: Look this isn't a debate, you fucking are not, you are not even thinking about it, you hear me? Manni…? Right I've had it with him, I'm having him, I'm not having him fuck your life up, that's my job.

MANNI: What you gonna do?

LOU: Good slapping, I'll deck him too. Then I'll really give him something to cry about, I'll fuck him. I'll slap him and then I'll fuck him. I'll slap him while I'm fucking him.

MANNI: Oh, right…go on then.

LOU: Right!

LOUISE starts to make her way out of flat, still carrying on.

I'll make his fucking arse drop I will.

LOUISE leaves, we hear front door open and slam shut. MANNI takes quick swig of vodka. Starts to put cap back on. Nodding.

MANNI: I know now.

We hear front door open and slowly close. LOUISE appears in doorway.

LOU: Where is he?

MANNI: Gone home.

LOU: …ph…phooey…

MANNI: Looks like tomorrow's the night then.

LOU: What for?

MANNI: Well if Mehir don't want it I'm sure there must be plenty of others who do.

LOU: Don't be daft.

MANNI: Someone really nice? You sort it out for me?

LOU: No, I won't.

MANNI: You said – why not? What is this? I can't please you no matter what I –

LOU: I don't want you to please me, please yourself!

MANNI: I will.

LOU: Manni, just tell Mehir to go jump and go look round Kent right? Just go. Please… You mind if I sleep on fold-up?

MANNI: Don't you wanna talk crap? Watch sun come up?

LOU: Fuck the sun.

LOUISE staggers over to the fold-up and sprawls out on it. MANNI takes another little blanket from wardrobe and puts it over LOUISE, switches light off and sits on bed a moment. There's only the orange street-light glow coming in.

Scene 6

Mid-morning.

The fold-up bed has been folded up and is lying unused against table. This is the morning after a really heavy night's drinking.

MANNI (in her black clubbing dress) is lying on top of a heaped duvet, her dress is rucked-up about her middriff, bum and knickers sticking up.

LOUISE (in one of her clubbing dresses) is under the bit of duvet MANNI hasn't got.

One of LOUISE's hands sticks out resting squarely on MANNI's knickers and bum.

Under the duvet LOUISE stirs, her head appears, looking around dazed. Sees her hand on MANNI's bum.

LOU: Ahhh!

She whisks hand away, sitting bolt upright kind of freaked back against wall breathing heavily for a moment. MANNI doesn't stir. LOUISE looks round room completely lost and confused. She's looking for anything to look at except MANNI and turns to the window, where she is dazed by daylight.

Oh…phooey.

Bracing herself LOUISE pulls bit of curtain aside to sneak a look outside again. She sits at side of window looking round room unimpressed, settles back on MANNI. Looks at watch – horrified, then at MANNI and back at watch trying to believe the time.

With urgency LOUISE tries to find somewhere to tap MANNI that isn't her bum. Shakes her by shoulder.

Manni… Manni… Manni it nearly eleven.

MANNI: Huh?

LOU: You awake?

MANNI: Uh?

LOU: It weren't today were it?

MANNI: What?

LOU: Your trip to Kent, it weren't today were it?

MANNI: What?

LOU: Your trip to Kent, it weren't today were it?

MANNI: Yeah.

LOU: What time were your train?

MANNI: Eight.

LOU: Oh fuck. Manni it's eleven.

MANNI: Oh, don't matter.

LOU: What you mean it don't matter? Course it matters!

MANNI: A-hu.

LOU: You even wanna go? …Well you couldn't have gone like this. Why didn't you say last night 'stead of letting me buy yer drinks? Why didn't you fucking say?… Manni? …Manni?

MANNI: Uh?

LOU: Manni!

LOUISE reaches over to bedside for cigarettes and lighter. Lights cig and settles back against wall, constantly worried and shaking head.

You should have bloody well said.

MANNI: I did say, you didn't listen.

MANNI starts to stir, writhe almost as if in pain. MANNI puts a hand out and waves it about. Hand stops and MANNI sticks her head up to look at hand.

…cold.

MANNI groans and puts one hand on floor. Leans out and puts other hand on floor, constantly groaning. Eases one leg out onto floor. Supporting hands stagger a few feet forward so the remaining leg is dragged from the duvet. MANNI is there on all fours, head down. Groggy and groaning.

…Never…felt like…

LOU: Like what?

MANNI: …Like this…

LOU: You never got that pissed before. Even by my standards. You not far from stomach pump you daft mare.

MANNI: What on fuck on God's earth did you make us drink?

LOU: I didn't make you.

MANNI: You did.

LOU: Alright I did, but not that much I didn't.

MANNI: Did – what on…fuck…hate you, HATE YOU!

This brings on potential chunder wave she has to ride out, LOUISE watches frightened and upset by how much MANNI is hungover.

What was it?

LOU: Dunno.

MANNI: What was it?

LOU: Baileys, Baileys an' something.

MANNI: …Hu?

LOU: That…and something…it made the cream curdle. Sort of cheesey pint.

MANNI: Hate you. I mean it, I do I hate you.

LOU: You do. All I do. Get you pissed.

MANNI: I'm going to die.

LOU: Manni, what you trying to do here? Where you going?

MANNI crawls forward a little and stops, starts to cry, then stops herself… LOUISE shudders under every tear.

MANNI: I've told Mehir.

LOU: Aye, I know you did. You want bog?

MANNI: Aye, that be nice.

MANNI gives a big groan and LOUISE quickly gets off bed to comfort her. LOUISE tries to help her up. MANNI really doesn't want to.

No no no no no no no…

LOU: No?

MANNI: Lea' me! Lea' me!

LOU: You want bowl then?

MANNI: Hu.

LOUISE staggers to get the plastic tub which she places under MANNI's mouth.

LOU: I saw Mehir crying.

MANNI: Were he?

LOU: Buckets. What you say?

MANNI: I didn't mean to. An' I said no right nice and polite but he kept on an' on bugging me, an' I were dancing on me tod happy, right happy on me tod I were an' I thought I were mad for him an' he still bugging me – so I said go fuck yerself up yer arse yer sad twat.

LOU: Weren't that bit of an overreaction?

MANNI: He wouldn't take hint though an' I were on me tod, dancing, I'm happy.

LOUISE switches light on, harsh light.

Ahhh! Off! Off off off off off –

LOUISE: Alright alright!

LOUISE switches light back off and sits on floor next to the all-fours MANNI, rubs her back.

That helping?

MANNI: Bit.

LOU: You want cig?

MANNI: Aye, aye I do. Quick, quick!

LOU: Hang on, gimme –

MANNI: Now!

LOU: Alright!

MANNI: Don't light it, just taste.

LOU: You and yer psychology.

LOUISE takes her cig and sticks it in MANNI's mouth.

There, chew on that.

MANNI: I don't want to chunder.

LOU: What you put away you no chance of that.

MANNI: You got work?

LOU: Aye. You be alright on yer own?

MANNI: No. Don't go.

LOU: Manni! I gotta!

MANNI: I don't wanna chunder. Not on me own.

LOU: You got to.

MANNI: It gonna burn, burn me throat and me mouth, burn me.

LOU: Bring it on then, two fingers an' –

MANNI: Louise!

LOU: Why'd you tell him night before yer trip?

MANNI: Why you get me pissed?

LOU: Why you let me get you? I thought you wanted to go on this trip?

MANNI: I don't care. You doing alright, got job. Doing Wakey.

LOU: But that not you.

MANNI: Fucked off with it Lou, with Mehir, wi' college, I not going back after hols…time out alright? Year out – do Wakey.

LOU: Chuffing losing it Manni.

LOUISE gives up and shivers (because she's still in the clubbing dress) and clambers back under duvet, sitting against wall. Commotion as she loses cigarette and has to find it within duvet. Resurfaces, slapping a bit of duvet down where she thinks it might be burning.

MANNI: What?

LOU: Nothing.

MANNI: Burnt duvet 'gain?

LOU: …Manni?

MANNI: Yeah?

LOU: Tonight, can I wear one of yours?

MANNI: My what?

LOU: Dresses?

MANNI: …Yeah, sure.

MANNI starts to retch quite badly. LOUISE scrambles from bed to comfort her, one arm round shoulder, other rubbing back.

LOU: Sssssshhh. Come on, come on.

It takes a moment but MANNI calms down and comes through it.

You gonna hurt yer'self. You gotta learn how to pace yourself.

LOUISE sits back on floor and looks up at window sadly.

I gotta get ready for work.

MANNI: No no no no no. Don't leave me.

LOU: I got to.

Unsure LOUISE goes out of room, looking back at MANNI. Moment passes, we hear water running. MANNI suddenly staggers up and leaves room. LOUISE re-enters, having been turfed out of bathroom. Sits on bed as we hear MANNI beeing sick and retching. LOUISE stares round room until her eyes settle on the glossy uni brochures.

She picks them up and fingers through them, genuinely looking at the pages in extreme detail until she snaps and hurls them across the room, yelling after them –

Go on then! Go fuck it all up Manni I aren't stopping you or fuck off and go!

Go to fucking uni! Whatever you do you gonna lea' me aren't you?

MANNI staggers back into room, supporting herself in doorway, wiping mouth with bare arm.

MANNI: You what?

LOUISE goes and picks up the thrown brochure, puts it back on table.

LOU: I don't want you to go neither. Ever.

LOUISE returns to bathroom leaving MANNI to pick bowl up and place it by the bed, laying on bed with her head by edge facing near to the bowl – just in case.

Scene 7

Late evening.

We hear front door opening and being slammed shut.

LOUISE (in one of MANNI's little black dresses) is huddled by side of bed tearful and shaken, arms wrapped round herself. One of the dress straps is broken and hanging loose off her shoulder. LOUISE sees broken strap and tries to put it back in place. It falls away, it's broken.

MANNI appears in doorway, freaked and shaken but not tearful.

MANNI: You alright? …He's gone…good I came back when I…you alright Lou? He didn't hurt you did he? Did he?

LOU: …No.

MANNI: Don't look it.

LOU: I don't feel it.

MANNI: Don't believe it, I were…I were dancing with that bastard. I thought he were nice and then he disappeared on me…and he nearly…you…lucky me coming back like that weren't it? Lou… Weren't it Lou? Lou?

LOU: Good thing you coming back.

MANNI: I would come and gi' you hug like but if I did… don't think I could…together, keep it together like.

LOU: You alright?

Suddenly MANNI rushes to the sink and we hear her throwing up and then retching, stays bent over sink a moment as she regains control, gasping for breath…calming down.

MANNI: So this is what brave feels like…I don't like it.

MANNI turns from sink and slides down cupboard onto bum, hands to face for a moment.

I want to go home.

LOUISE picks herself up and staggers over to MANNI, puts hand out to lift her up. MANNI looks away. LOUISE crouches down to face MANNI. MANNI gets up and stumbles past LOUISE to slump against the bed. MANNI swipes vodka

bottle off bedside, fumbles with cap and tries to take swig.
Gags on vodka and spurts it back out. Coughs, bent down.
For a moment LOUISE can't bear to look at her. MANNI
composes herself a little, stands and walks round room a little
as if trying to keep busy before settling back down a few feet
from LOUISE.

LOU: He wouldn't have done ought.

MANNI: Aye, his arse dropped when I came in didn't it? I
may not be able to pull 'em but I can sure make 'em
cack their pants. Scream scream scream scream scream!
Wouldn't have missed that for world. Get out! Get out!…
You owe me one, all those drinks you bought me are
scrubbed, we even me and you.

MANNI notices broken dress on LOUISE.

Fucker's ripped me dress!

LOUISE looks at MANNI who points back at her. LOUISE
sees broken straps again, tries to put it back in place. It falls
down again.

LOU: It'll…it'll…

MANNI: It'll what?

LOU: Sew back. It'll sew back.

MANNI: It bloody will.

LOU: He were so nice in club Manni. He really was.

MANNI: But you said you weren't gonna be tonight you
said, wearing my dress.

LOU: …Just happened.

MANNI: No, why? Why him of all gits you could a' had. I
were dancing wi' him an' all. Bastard like but I were
dancing wi' him… Lou? Did you? You didn't –

LOU: Aye. Soz, I'm sorry but I know that one Manni. I saw he were gonna pull you – you! I know what he's like an' I know he's always fancied you an' you you daft cow were all over him…you weren't going with him. Not yer first time.

MANNI: 'Cos of me?

LOU: Not with him you weren't, not your first time – NO!

MANNI gets near LOUISE, wants to put hand out to comfort her but can't, both too on edge.

I'm sorry but I couldn't think of ought else to…he wouldn't have done ought to me. I'd have got him to stop. He would have listened.

MANNI: Lou, he were pissed.

LOU: How could you tell? It just went bit out of control and when I said…no he…wouldn't stop. He wouldn't…

MANNI: Did he hurt you?

LOU: I think he were gonna.

MANNI takes huge swig from vodka.

Manni stop it! Stop it!

MANNI breaks off from her swig.

MANNI: What? Thought this was how you liked me?

MANNI takes another swig.

LOU: Stop it!

MANNI is trying to think of a response, frustrated and just gives LOUISE the finger gesture. MANNI slumps back. LOUISE looks at strap again.

Don't think it'll sew back proper.

MANNI: God. Lets gets pissed…oh, we already doing that, shit.

Silence. Only the muffled competing music.

MANNI gets up and climbs into bed, pulls duvet tight round her facing away from LOUISE. LOUISE watches her a moment and then goes to light switch. Turns light off and room is plunged into darkness bar the orange light trying to get through the curtains.

Time passes and the music outside fades to nothing. Quiet. Late at night. Though she can barely be seen LOUISE is sat on floor in doorway.

Lou?…Lou? Lou, where are you?

LOU: Over here.

MANNI: You not in bed? Where?

LOU: Here.

MANNI: Still? Come on get in, you catch yer cold there.

LOU: I'm alright.

MANNI: I haven't got monk on or ought on with you.

We hear MANNI shuffling about and then opening the curtains and the window slightly. The room is lit by the orange street-lights beaming into the room. LOUISE is sat in doorway lifeless.

Air in here gets right manky doesn't it?

LOU: Yeah.

MANNI sits on end of bed looking at her friend who is clearly upset, but both manage to smile at each other.

MANNI: Get in here, get yourself warm aye?

LOU: I'm alright.

MANNI: Might be summer but I still miss double glazing. Miss extra lining curtains in me room have.

LOU: Yeah.

MANNI: Come winter gonna be cold here.

LOUISE pushes herself up and goes stands by bed, looks out through window onto street.

LOU: I shouldn't have brought you here.

MANNI: Shurrrup. What you like?

LOU: No, I shouldn't. All I wanted at school was be up Wakey. Nought else mattered and on Mondays I told you what it were like yer mouth used to hang open all droopy drawers like, I loved that. Had you in palm of me hand. I spun you right load of old crap…but I believed it too so…an' you thought I were so smart, you…you who've always known where you going. What have me and you got in common apart from sitting next to each other at school?

MANNI: We have a laugh. We had right laugh at school.

LOU: But we not at school no more. All I wanted since school is do Wakey. Wakey Wakey Wakey…all I got is doing Wakey.

MANNI: But you like Wakey.

LOU: But that all there is. I can't just do Wakey, it don't mean ought like this.

MANNI: What you saying? You want to do Leeds?

LOU: …Manni, Manni… This place were so special to me. It's dead to me. Just dead waiting to come alive to get you, the one right good thing in my life fucked over. This place were so special.

MANNI: Still is.

LOU: No. I bash specialness out of everything I do. Wakey, you…and I still drag 'em up here or into bogs and…no specialness.

LOUISE goes and sits back in doorway.

MANNI: …Lou, I'm only telling you this cos…cos I'm stupid right? But last night, cheesey pint night, you were stretching and your hand wandered onto me, didn't it?

LOU: Aye. Sorry.

MANNI: Aye, I'd told him no, but when you touched me I couldn't stop me'self 'magining it were his hand touching me.

LOU: Oh.

MANNI: You gonna kill me aren't you?

LOU: …No.

MANNI: But you see Mehir's touch were fine but, fine to describe touch of love of your life, cos after a while it were yer hand again, me best mate, meant more, that were special, to me…and I'm not a fucking lesbian, alright?

LOU: No.

MANNI: No.

LOU: Thank you.

MANNI: You freaked when you saw where yer hand were. What you like? You freaked?

LOU: Waste of money that fold-up weren't it?

MANNI: Aye.

LOU: I need to stretch, I'm not sure this is healthy.

MANNI: What isn't?

LOU: Me and you mate. We done Wakey, we done it fine, but we nowhere left to go.

MANNI: Haven't we?

LOU: No…don't kill me but, I been to see me Mam. To see if I could go home.

MANNI: Oh. How'd it go?

LOU: …She said no.

MANNI: No?

LOU: No. Never occurred to me she'd say no.

MANNI: No.

LOU: She said life were lot quieter wi'out me…but I can pop round for me Sunday dinner if I like…Sunday dinner? She me Mam, she not meant to say no. I ended up begging her. Right begging I was. Humiliating. An' she still said get on with it. She's meant to love me.

MANNI: Oh Lou.

LOU: I stuck here…can you see me begging me Mam?

MANNI: You just gotta give her bit of time. It's cos she's hurt cos you haven't been in touch and stuff. Leave it few days and try again aye? She change.

LOU: She won't change.

MANNI: She will. She'll calm down. She's nice your Mam, she won't turn you away.

LOU: It's time you went home.

MANNI: I can't, you're still here.

LOU: Go home.

MANNI: Who are you to tell me to go home? You said come here you did. On and on you went. Desperate to get away from home you were.

LOU: Everywhere's just next place to get away from.

MANNI: Well I'm staying. If you can't go home then neither can I.

LOU: Well stop getting gippy then! Lose your job and you won't have any choice. They'll sack you.

MANNI: Get another.

LOU: Manni, just go home aye?

MANNI: I'm not leaving you. You need me here.

LOU: I bloody don't. You know what you do? You depress hell outta me you do…

MANNI: Well I need you.

LOU: Manni, please.

MANNI: You wouldn't leave me.

LOU: I won't mind. I'll understand.

MANNI: What would you do?

LOU: I'd find somewhere, I'd think of something. It's not your problem. Might keep this place on, get more hours I manage it.

MANNI: That isn't gonna help you.

LOU: Well forget about me. You're throwing yourself away for fuck all here. Go home.

MANNI: Ask yer Mam again.

LOU: She won't let me back in, I tried.

MANNI: Try again.

LOU: I have!

MANNI: Well try harder.

LOU: You didn't see me, I did try!

MANNI: No you didn't cos you're still here. Don't you want to go home?

LOUISE nods.

Then you're gonna have to beg some more.

LOU: I can't…are you going to do yer shift tomorrow?

MANNI: If I not gippy like.

LOU: They sack you this time.

MANNI: …Why don't you get in here? You must be cold. I'm not a lesbian.

LOU: I'm alright here.

MANNI: Sleep tight Lou.

Giving in, MANNI settles back down. LOUISE stays sat in doorway.

Scene 8

Early evening.

We hear front door open and LOUISE (casual clothes) enters with huge bags of laundry. Leaves them by side of bed and flops down on it for a moment. Sits back up, drawn, exhausted.

Picks up vodka bottle from side of bed and looks at it almost contemptuously before leaving it on table. LOUISE sits on bed looking onto street as we hear door open and MANNI enters (casual clothes). MANNI stands in doorway still a bit hung-over and distracted.

MANNI: Did they sack me?

LOU: Yeah… Where you been?

MANNI: Walk. Fresh air. Sober up.

LOU: You must have been gone ages, I finished work hours ago.

MANNI: I have. Been thinking. I gonna pace me'self proper from now on…what you been doing?

LOU: Laundry. Done yours too.

MANNI: You didn't have to.

LOU: I wanted to. Good places to think launderettes… Manni, I'm going home.

MANNI: You are?

LOU: Me stuff's already gone.

MANNI: It all sorted with yer Mam then?

LOU: Yeah…

MANNI looks away, out of window a moment.

MANNI: Right, well good. You told landlord?

LOU: Aye. Landlord says us girls never stay long. We all paid up wi' him so thought I'd get it over with. Me stuff's already gone.

MANNI: You said.

LOU: Your Mam an' Dad let you back in won't they?

MANNI: Aye, open arms.

LOU: Thought so…I didn't know where you'd gone. I just brought your laundry back.

MANNI: Right.

LOU: Say goodbye.

MANNI: Goodbye? We don't have to go just yet do we? Don't you fancy one last night up Wakey?

LOU: We done Wakey.

Quiet. A long awkward pause where they avoid looking at each other. Eyes finally meet.

You going back to college proper then? .

MANNI: Never left really, not official like so…what you been doing?

LOU: I gonna try an' be a holiday rep. I been looking into it.

MANNI: Have you?

LOU: Aye. I got me own brochures I have, to look through. You not only one wi' brochures.

MANNI: How long you been thinking that?

LOU: Few days, only an idea but I'm dead keen. What you think?

MANNI: Yeah!

LOU: New places. New people.

MANNI: Yeah.

LOU: Me Dad says can lead to career in management, gets carried away right easy me Dad.

MANNI: Dads do.

LOU: We still friends aren't we?

MANNI: Course we are, what make you think we not?

LOU: Just…everything.

MANNI: No.

LOU: I mean, I mean you'll think of me as a friend won't you?

MANNI: Course I will.

LOU: We were good mates.

MANNI: Still are. Untouchable like.

LOU: You keep in touch?

MANNI: Will you?

LOU: …Oh yeah.

MANNI: We'll leave it a while yeah?

LOU: Yeah.

MANNI: And then 'fore I go to uni we do Leeds for night, do it large like we always said we would.

LOU: I'll give you a call.

MANNI: I'll give you a call.

LOU: We all done then?

MANNI: Reckon so.

LOU: You still gotta pack.

MANNI: Aye.

LOU: Best leave you to it.

MANNI: Aye.

LOUISE takes her key out and lays it on table.

LOU: Hate you.

MANNI: Hate you more.

LOU: Hate you more.

LOUISE hurries out.

MANNI looks round room lost. For a brief moment she is nearly tearful, then pulls herself together. Looks out of window a moment and then pulls suitcase out from under bed. Opens it and starts to pack laundry clothes into it. Stops. Sees vodka bottle on table and picks it up eyeing the tiny bit left. Opens it and swigs the last drop away. Puts bottle in bin.

MANNI: Aye, we're done.

MANNI returns to packing her clothes.

The End.